Brown As an Acorn

Marrón como una bellota

written by **Molly Dingles**

illustrated by **Walter Velez**

dingles&company New Jersey

First printing

PUBLISHED BY dingles&company
P.O. Box 508 • Sea Girt, New Jersey • 08750
WEBSITE: www.dingles.com • E-MAIL: info@dingles.com

Library of Congress Catalog Card No.: 2004091477
ISBN: 1-891997-37-8

Printed in the United States of America

●

ART DIRECTED & DESIGNED BY Barbie Lambert

DESIGN ASSISTANT Erin Collity

ENGLISH EDITED BY Andrea Curley SPANISH EDITED BY John Page

EDUCATION CONSULTANT Kathleen P. Miller

PREPRESS BY Pixel Graphics, Inc.

For Skip & Janine

Molly Dingles

is the author of *Jinka Jinka Jelly Bean* and *Little Lee Lee's Birthday Bang*. As Judy Zocchi, she has written the *Paulie & Sasha* series. She is a writer and lyricist who holds a bachelor's degree in fine arts/theater from Mount Saint Mary's College and a master's degree in educational theater from New York University. She lives in Manasquan, New Jersey, with her husband, David.

Walter Velez

was born in New York. He attended the High School of Art and Design and later the School of Visual Arts. He has done illustration work for many major book and gaming companies. He is known for the popular series *Thieves World* as well as the *Myth* series for Ace Books. He has also produced trading cards for *Goosebumps* and *Dune*. In addition, Walter has illustrated several *Star Wars* books for Random House. He lives in Queens, New York, with his wife, Kriti, and daughter, Kassandra.

The Community of Color series is more than just a series of books about colors. The series demonstrates how individual people, places, and things combine to form a community. It allows children to view the world in segments and then experience the wonderment and value of the community as a whole.

Brown as a cabin

Marrón
como una cabaña

Brown loaf of bread

Barra de pan marrón

Brown as a chipmunk

Marrón como
una ardilla listada

Brown bird to be fed

Pájaro marrón
que alimentar

Brown as a beaver

Marrón como un castor

Brown chocolate cake

Pastel de chocolate marrón

Brown as an acorn

Marrón como una bellota

Brown dock in the lake

Muelle marrón en el lago

Brown as a mud pie

Marrón como
una tortita de barro

Brown icy tea

Té marrón helado

Brown as a squirrel

●

Marrón como una ardilla

Brown trunk of a tree

Tronco marrón
de un árbol

The color Brown
is all around.

El color Marrón está
en todas partes.

Where at this camp can Brown be found?

¿En qué parte de este campamento se puede encontrar el color Marrón?

ABOUT COLOR

Use the Community of Color series to teach your child to identify the most basic colors and to help him or her relate these colors to objects in the real world. ASK:

- What color is this book about?
- Can you name the brown things in this camp?
- Can you find a brown chipmunk in this picture?
- What brown dessert is in this picture?

ABOUT COMMUNITY

Use the Community of Color series to teach your child how he or she is an important part of the community. Explain to your child what a community is.

- A community is a place where people live, work, and play together.
- Your family is a community.
- Your school is a community.
- Your neighborhood is a community.
- The world is one big community.

Everyone plays an important part in making a community work - moms, dads, boys, girls, police officers, firefighters, teachers, mail carriers, garbage collectors, store clerks, and even animals are all important parts of a community. USE THESE QUESTIONS TO FURTHER THE CONVERSATION:

- How are the people at this camp interacting with one another?
- How are the people different from one another? How are they the same?
- What do they have in common?
- How is the community you see in this book like your community? How is it different?
- Describe your community.

ABOUT FEELINGS

Colors can describe as well as evoke different emotions. Encourage your child to describe the feelings that the color brown inspires.

- How does the color brown make you feel?
- Name your favorite brown thing in this book. Why is it your favorite?
- Name your favorite brown thing at home. Why is it your favorite?
- Can you tell how the people in the picture feel by looking at their faces?
  Do you ever feel the same way? When? Why?

TRY SOMETHING NEW... Help those in need! With your parents help, have an ice-tea stand and donate the money you earn to a charity of your choice.

community of color series